# FUSION

BRIDGING THE GAP BETWEEN CIVIL RIGHTS & HIP-HOP

DR. BENJAMIN F. CHAVIS JR. & MC LYTE

| | |
|---|---|
| Publisher: | Sunni Gyrl, Inc. |
| Publisher Address: | 14431 Ventura Blvd #120 |
| Publisher City, State, Zip: | Sherman Oaks, CA 91423 |
| Website: | www.sunnigyrl.com |
| Phone: | 855.625.9831 |
| ISBN 13: | 978-0-9773232-5-8 |

| | |
|---|---|
| Graphic Design: | Jacob Leshaa |
| Editors: | Lynn Richardson |
| | Lisa Bennett |

# DEDICATION

All that I write, utter and all that we share in this publication are the results of the contributions and aspirations of millions of people who yearn and cry out for a better quality of life. In addition to the people, organizations and movements that have helped over the past years to make possible the special collaboration that <u>Fusion</u> exemplifies and represents.

First and foremost, I acknowledge that there is only one God, the Creator and

Liberator of the world. Known by many different names in many different languages, religions and cultures, there is only one God. That is why I affirm the oneness of God and the oneness of humanity.

Secondly, I acknowledge the Chavis family. Our family is but one of millions of families that are representative of the long struggle of humanity for freedom, justice and equality. From before the days of my great-great grandfather, The Reverend John Chavis (1762-1838), in Granville County and

Oxford, North Carolina to numerous cities and counties across the United States, in Africa and in the Caribbean, the Chavis family in 2015 continues to speak out and stand up for the liberation of humanity from the domestic and global tentacles of oppression and injustice.

I will always be grateful to my father, Benjamin F. Chavis, Sr., and my mother Elisabeth Ridley Chavis, for nurturing me and guiding me to join the Civil Rights Movement at the age of 12. My sisters: June Chavis Davenport, Dr. Helen Chavis

Othow, and Dr. La Rhoda Francine Chavis all were instrumental in the evolution of my consciousness and activism. I wholeheartedly thank my wife, Martha Rivera Chavis, and my children: Michele, Paula, Benjamin III, Renita, Franklin, Ana, John and Reginald, grandchildren and great grandchildren for all their encouragement.

Salute and recognition is more than warranted to my codefendants in the triumphant 40-year old civil rights case, The Wilmington Ten: Wayne Moore,

Marvin Patrick, James McKoy, Willie Earl Vereen, Reginald Epps, Ann Shepard, William "Joe" Wright, Jerry Jacobs and Connie Tindall.

Organizational acknowledgements include: The National Association for the Advancement of Colored People (NAACP), Dr. Martin Luther King, Jr. and the Southern Christian Leadership Conference (SCLC), Dr. Charles E. Cobb, Sr. and the United Church of Christ (UCC) Commission for Racial Justice (CRJ), UCC "Civil Rights Journal," Ministers for Racial and Social Justice (MRSJ), United Black Christians (UBC), National Conference of Black Churchmen (NCBC), Black Theology Project, National Council of Churches of USA, Council of Churches of Republic of Cuba, World Council of Churches, Nelson Mandela and the African National Congress (ANC), Popular Movement for the Liberation of Angola (MPLA), South West African People's Organization (SWAPO), National Alliance Against Racist and Political Repression (NAARPR), African Liberation Day National

Committee, Wilmington Ten Defense Committee, National African American Leadership Summit (NAALS), Million Man March National Committee, Nation of Islam (NOI), Phi Beta Sigma Fraternity, Prince Hall Masons, Def Jam Recordings, Russell Simmons and Rush Communications, Rush Philanthropic Arts Foundation, Hip-Hop Summit Action Network (HSAN), Diamond Empowerment Fund (DEF), Women in Entertainment Empowerment Network (WEEN), Hip-Hop Caucus, Foundation for Ethnic

Understanding, United Nations, WOL Radio "Freedom Journal," Education Online Services Corporation, National Association for Equal Opportunity in Higher Education (NAFEO), and the National Newspaper Publishers Association (NNPA).

Academic acknowledgements include: Saint Augustine's University, University of North Carolina at Charlotte, Duke University School of Divinity, Howard University School of Religion and Union Theological Seminary.

I must finally acknowledge my publicist Lisa Bennett, my HSAN associate co-executive Lynn Richardson and, of course, MC Lyte who is my gifted co-author of this unique book, <u>Fusion</u>.

We all have work together hopefully to present another useful literary offering to the world.

# *INSIDE FUSION*

# *FOREWORD*
## *DR. BENJAMIN F. CHAVIS JR*

Fusion is the timely literary convergence between MC Lyte and me. It is a mixed tape utilizing our writing pens mutually dedicated to explicating the living connection, relevance and the cultural evolution of the relationship between Hip-Hop and the Civil Rights Movement in America. We resonate together speaking truth to power.

Working with MC Lyte has been and continues to be a special blessing. It is simply a sacred honor to coauthor this book with MC Lyte. We hope the content will stimulate a better understanding of both the cultural phenomena of Hip-Hop and the consciousness and activism of the freedom struggle and movement not only in the United States but also throughout the world where people demand freedom, justice and equality.

As a 50-year veteran of the movement that contributed to advancing the cause of human dignity and freedom, I recognized early on that Hip-Hop represented the cognitive and artistic genius of a generation of young freedom fighters who would continue to push forward to improve the quality of life of all people. Hip-Hop demands equal justice and pulls the sheets off of the profanity of poverty.

Our poetry, music, songs, dance, artwork, and videos are no longer at the margins of society, but are now at the core of the mindset of an intergenerational, multicultural, multilingual and international movement for freedom and justice. Fusion shares our dialogue, dreams and determination to keeping spitting truth.

MC Lyte and I are part of a progressive team of innovators and activists. The best form of expression is self-expression. We cannot afford a cultural or a generational gap. We, therefore, invite you to join us on the journey to change our world for the betterment of all humanity. Let us hear from you. Let your voice be heard and felt. Let us all be in a resolute solidarity with each other.

# *FOREWORD*
# *MC LYTE*

My love for Hip Hop is not easily explainable. While I will always claim my rightful place simply because of the contributions I've been blessed to share, the genre pushes me to connect today's happenings with truthful lyrics that depict the actual scene of the community. Hip Hop has been my saving grace. It has built me up and given me a platform where my voice can be heard and appreciated.

I honor the Hip Hop Movement whole heartedly and depend upon it's forerunners to continue to educate and broaden the minds of the youth.

This opportunity to unite with Dr. Ben, for this body of work, is truly like no other. I respect Dr. Ben's tireless efforts and commitment to his people. His strength and courage exemplify what it will take moving into the next few decades as we fight for position to attain and reestablish responsibility, respect, fortitude, and dignity within our global community.

Dr Ben and I hold fast to the concept that keeping generations interlocked is of great importance. We represent leadership in two different sectors of our culture that dare not be separated.

# THE CONVERSATION

**MC Lyte**: Wow! Doc I wanted to ask you something. Just being someone who's experienced hip-hop not as an emcee, but you know, you're in it, but then you hover above; So you're able to see things that are occurring that we might not even see while we're in it. What do you think over the years has been lost or gained in hip-hop?

**Dr. Chavis**: Well, first let me just say I'm always honored to be in your presence.

**MC Lyte**: Thank you Doc. Same here.

**Dr. Chavis**: Because I see the civil rights movement in you. I see fighting for freedom, justice, and equality in you. And you are an emcee; you are an icon in hip-hop. See . . . to me it's not just the connection; It is an evolution of our struggle, of our self-expression, of how we spit words or say poetry or lyrics or communicate.

**MC Lyte**: Communicate, yeah.

**Dr. Chavis**: And it's not a lot of what we hear but what we feel. Because when you are MC Lyte, it's not only what is heard, but what's felt. Similarly, when I worked with the Rev Dr. Martin Luther King Jr. as a young teenager, I heard my man but I also felt my man.

**MC Lyte**: Yeah, yeah.

**Dr. Chavis**: You know. It's one thing to hear about the dream, it's another thing to feel it. You feel it before you get it.

**MC Lyte**: Okay.

**Dr. Chavis**: When they sang "We Shall Overcome," we weren't overcoming, but we sang "We Shall Overcome" like we were overcoming.

**MC Lyte**: This brings me to the Wilmington 10. Tell us what was that experience like.

**Dr. Chavis**: Well, it was a somewhat painful experience. But in the end, there were trials; and you have to go through that storm to be able to appreciate, eventually, winning, after 40 years of struggle with it.

The context was Dr. King was killed in April of 1968. This is three years later in 1971, Richard Nixon is the president of the United States, they're still arguing over school desegregation in my home state of North Carolina, Port City Wilmington. There was a whole struggle about whether or not black kids can go to school with white kids and whether or not white kids can go to schools with black kids; Whether there would be some equity of consideration, whether there would be some equality of what was offered particularly to black kids...there was always that inequity, even though the Brown decision of the Supreme Court in 1954 said unequal schools was unconstitutional. Unequal and separate were unconstitutional.

**MC Lyte**: But they were still…

**Dr. Chavis**: They were still you know…they found a way to get around the law.

**MC Lyte**: Don't they always?

**Dr. Chavis**: Always. And so in 1971, the United Church of Christ commissioned for racial justice. I was a minister for the United Church of Christ. They sent me to Wilmington as a young organizer. I was 23 years old.

**MC Lyte**: Okay.

**Dr. Chavis**: But even though I was 23, I was a veteran organizer because I started out when I was 12 or 13.

**MC Lyte**: Ok. Ha.

**Dr. Chavis**: So I was . . . so I was a 10-year veteran.

**MC Lyte**: Wait a minute. At 12 and13 what were you organizing?

**Dr. Chavis**: I was the statewide youth coordinator for the Southern Christian Leadership Conference. In other words, I was the statewide youth leadership coordinator, when I was 12. . . 13 . . . 14 for Reverend Dr. Martin Luther King Jr. That was my assignment.

**MC Lyte**: Right.

**Dr. Chavis**: You know, I was writing editorials for the Carolina Times when I was 12 . . . 11 years old . . . with the pen.

**MC Lyte**: So that right there....

**Dr. Chavis**: So writing lyrics, writing, expressing yourself...

**MC Lyte**: Yeah.

**Dr. Chavis**: Self-expression, that's part of what the movement was all about.

**MC Lyte**: Well, I'm just thinking now. . . you're saying

12, 13. . . that's a lot of responsibility. Do you think that responsibility lacks now with kids?

**Dr. Chavis**: I think it's a matter of consciousness. I was very conscious of what racial discrimination was when I was 5 . . . 6 . . . 7. So keep in mind, I couldn't wait. I thought I was grown by the time I was 12 and 13.

**MC Lyte**: Okay.

**Dr. Chavis**: But the consciousness started way before

then. So we have to get our young people, not just when they are teenagers, you have to get our young people now. I've never heard of people being expelled from pre-K. We got some very young brothers and sisters getting expelled from pre-K.

**MC Lyte**: From pre-K, yeah.

**Dr. Chavis**: So the consciousness has to start very very early. The earlier you start your self-awareness or self-consciousness about who you are and what kind of world we're living in and what is my role, what is our participation and that's why -- even though I am a veteran of the civil rights movement -- I was an early advocate of hip-hop.

**MC Lyte**: Okay.

**Dr. Chavis:** 'Cause I saw the connection. I didn't see this thing about post- civil rights and…

**MC Lyte**: What was your first hip-hop record?

**Dr. Chavis**: My first hip-hop record… It was Kurtis Blow.

**MC Lyte**: Kurtis Blow.

**Dr. Chavis**: Yes.

**MC Lyte**: The Brakes?

**Dr. Chavis**: Yes. Kurtis Blow. You know.

**MC Lyte**: Ha

**Dr. Chavis**: And I felt that the lyrics of hip-hop were so self-expressive at a time when the larger society was trying to put a clamp down on the community. You know, the South Bronx, you know wasn't just for a *Fort*

*Apache designation*. The south Bronx was a crucible where brothers and sisters danced differently and moved and vibed differently, and I saw a connection even though this was up south. See, people say the civil rights movement was down-south but I think Malcolm X had it right, the south was anything south of the Canadian border; the whole country was the South, whether you're in LA or New York, that's the south also.

**MC Lyte**: Okay. What would be his reason for saying that, though?

**Dr. Chavis**: Because…

**MC Lyte**: If the United States is its own continent?

**Dr. Chavis**: Because Malcolm understood that racial discrimination, prejudice, exploitation transcends…

**MC Lyte**: Borders.

**Dr. Chavis**: …borders, transcends geographical considerations. And that's why he eventually evolved into seeing himself as a worldwide freedom fighter, not just as an American, all over the world.

**MC Lyte**: That's amazing. But wait. Okay, we…

**Dr. Chavis**: So, 1 to 10. So, you know, I'm an organizer. I was 1 in 23 and I went down and organized the high school students in Wilmington, North Carolina to fight against the racism in the schools. We start some marches. We had some teach-ins. You know, back in those days, "dapping" was going on. You know, a lot of my high school classmates were in

Vietnam and the Vietnam War and they would come back "dapping". "Dapping" was a form of communicating but also making a beat with your fist.

**MC Lyte**: on your body?

**Dr. Chavis:** *(Dr. Chavis begins beating a rhythm on his leg)* Oh yeah, on your body. You were sending a message . . . that was like fraternity, that was like brotherhood, expressing themselves. I was dapping with the young students . . . male and female. Wasn't just brothers. Sisters were also dapping.

Communicating. Being self-expressive. And what I've always said, I must be honest with you. One of the reasons why I stayed in the movement 24 hours a day was because there were some fine sisters in the movement.

**MC Lyte**: Is that right?

**Dr. Chavis**: Oh yeah! Oh yeah. It wasn't just brothers. You could not even get a real girlfriend if you were not a freedom fighter.

**MC Lyte**: Right, if you were just some ordinary dude.

**Dr. Chavis**: Sisters want you to have some consciousness on your mind.

**Lyte**: Right. What has happened to the celebration of beauty of the African-American woman?

*\*Break due to a vibrating phone\**

**Lyte**: So you were making mention of how many years in the ***crunks*** of the struggle, women were not trying to hear from the guys if they weren't in the struggle; if they weren't a part of some organization that was moving for change. What do you think has happened to the celebration of African-American women today? It seems like the most uncool to be.

**Dr. Chavis**: Well, I think that it's not only... I think the absence of celebrating the essence and the beauty and the abundance of what it means to be an African-American woman and have that one being paid tribute to by brothers. In fact, you couldn't call yourself a brother if you didn't have a sister. And I'm not just talking about a fraternal or maternal, I'm talking about in terms of respect. The whole

"Black Is Beautiful" was started with the endowment of saluting the Black woman.

**Lyte**: Absolutely.

**Dr. Chavis**: I mean the afro [hair style]... afros were worshipped.

**Lyte**: How often did you fall in love as a teen?

**Dr. Chavis**: Oh many times. Many times.

**Lyte**: Is that right?

**Dr. Chavis**: I mean, you know. Because to me part of one's humanity... when you realize there are forces out here trying to deny your humanity, it makes you a little bit more conscious to not only protect your humanity but to assert it. But, not to assert male over female in terms of domination, no, it was to uplift. You know. How can I be an African king and there's no African queen?

**Lyte**: Right.

**Dr. Chavis**: You know. It's how we work together. It's how we struggle together. And if you look at the civil rights movement, if you look at who's out there on the front lines, there were a lot of sisters. It wasn't just brothers. You know. And one of the things that I think about hip hop... and I'm so glad you started Hip Hop Sisters because to me that reminds brothers in hip hop . . .what is our role? We should be celebrating that. We should be opening doors for sisters to make a contribution to the evolution and to the expansion and to the global awareness of the culture.

**Lyte**: I think that hip hop sort of... I guess it's a reflection of the community and what's going on in the community and as I listen to hip hop now, it seems, at least what's portrayed on the front lines. I'm not talking about conscious rap that exists on the lower level, in the basement, or somewhere on the Internet, where you have to really search for it. I'm talking about the stuff that's promoted worldwide. It seems very selfish. It seems very, you know, everyone's out for themselves as opposed to us coming out in the time we did. We were closely connected more to the struggle, you know, to those years of having come out and through and still pushing forth. And because they're a little bit further away, the things that were important to know, history of what went down, that they're able to now disassociate themselves from community and from calling themselves a brother because that would mean that they would have to be a brother to a sister.

**Dr. Chavis**: Right. What I think… sometimes you know we say in hip-hop, "flipping the script." Well, I think the script has been doubly flipped.

**Lyte**: Okay.

**Dr. Chavis**: In other words, it's just not about now struggling against oppression and exploitation. We have to now struggle with self-denial, with self-destruction, with self-unconsciousness. And I think that is a struggle . . . its apart of the socialization. And I think that... I don't think that... I don't think there are unconscious rappers and conscious rappers. I just think that they're conscious about different things. *[Lyte chuckles and says "wow"]* Some rappers are conscious about strip clubs, and that's what they rap about. The beats come from that. And then there are others that are conscious about the ongoing liberation struggle even in 2014 and 2015.

**Lyte**: How do we get young people conscious?

**Dr. Chavis**: Well, I think it's a process ... first of all, no one is born conscious. It's a part of the socialization process. I think young people . . . to answer your question . . . become conscious over a period of time if they're exposed to it. If they have the right seeds planted in their mix. You know, I was born on a farm, and I learned something about cultivation. You know. Plant those seeds. But, its just not about planting them...you have to make sure they grow. So you have to cultivate them. You have to make sure the weeds don't choke the life out of the seeds.

**Lyte**: Mmmm. I was gonna ask do you think that the system, let's just call it that. The huge system that these records, new records of hip hop exist in... Do you think they understand the power of the seed? Or, right now, they're just putting out music because there's money to be made?

**Dr. Chavis**: No. I think it's becoming so materialistic that we may have lost our sense of . . . first . . . self-value, and the value of the product that we create. You know I'm in the studio all the time and I used to hang with the Dip Set all the time. I used to tell them . . . I'd say, "Hey man. At the end of the day we have to be... I will defend your right to have artistic freedom. But with freedom comes responsibility."

**Lyte**: Absolutely.

**Dr. Chavis**: You can't just throw anything out there in the environment. You have to be responsible for what you put out there in the environment. And quite frankly, every time we have this discussion, it kind of gets to them. It's not like they're aloof and, "Oh Doc I don't really wanna hear that." They do take time. But they have to also be shown that, I can make some money doing it the right way.

Everybody says I can make some money doing it the wrong way. But can you really thrive being a righteous, dedicated person that puts stuff out in the environment? The answer is yes. But, the popular myth out there is that you will be broke if you would do that. The popular myth is that "Oh if I turn on myself, turn on my people, turn on my woman, oh I'm gonna be rich." See that's part of the incorrectness of how... it's just not artists . . . but it's the industry, in terms of how things are pitched and how things are made an example. You know,

I'm a strong defender of hip-hop. When Russell [Simmons] and I started the Hip Hop Summit Action Network, what I was so pleased with was the artists themselves. They said the theme of HSAN will be "Taking Back Responsibility." We didn't come… the artists wanted to give back. Wanted to show that it wasn't all about what I can take from life or take from the world, but what can I give to the world.

**Lyte**: Yeah. I would feel like a… I got a chance to see a panel where Hank Shocklee, I think I was on the panel, and Hank

Shocklee made a riveting point and that was, that the younger guys in hip-hop today, they don't have the OG in the room the way that some of the other guys did growing up. And it's a possibility that they're too... they're spending too much time amongst their peers who know about the same as they do. And if in fact they were able to open up their world and have someone that was a little older . . . who knew a little something more . . . who could school them every now and then . . . it would sort of help to shape their worlds a little differently. How true do you think that is?

**Dr. Chavis**: Oh I think that's very true, but I would say you become an OG by first being a young G. You see what I'm saying? I'm an OG, but I wasn't born an OG. I became an OG through trials and tribulations. I have not always made the right decisions in life but when I realized I made a wrong decision, I tried to learn from that decision. I'd say "Ben you're not gonna do this again. You're gonna learn from that."

**Lyte**: Did you have older... Well, I imagine being a part of those organizations...

**Dr. Chavis**: Absolutely. Yeah. Martin Luther King Jr., Floyd McKissick. Golden Frinks. Charles Earl Cobb...my own mother and father. I had a lot of mentors—male and female. I had a lot of what I consider OGs. And now that I'm an OG, I have a responsibility. And Lyte what impresses me about you, you have that wisdom, but you're still young. I don't know what you're doing; You got the fountain of youth up in you because you're an icon, but you still have that youthful dynamic effervescence about you. You're still glowing.

**Lyte**: Thank you.

**Dr. Chavis**: And to me that's attractive and intergenerational… the struggle today is intergenerational. It's not just one generation. When I was the… I became the youngest person to head the NAACP and they had this thing "Passing the Torch." And I probably made some of my board members a little uncomfortable, but I told them in 1993, "Make sure the torch is still lit and we will keep it lit."

**Lyte**: Before you pass it.

**Dr. Chavis**: Don't be handing me something where the fire of vitality has been smothered. See what I'm saying? I mean pass that baton, pass that torch, but just don't hand it off. Give me some guidance. Where am I running? What's the goal? How do I know I won the race? Where's the finish line?

**Lyte**: Wait a minute. What if I'm not ready for that torch right now? Hold on. Pass it to them. Let me get myself ready. You know . . . 'cause the worst thing is to be put in a position of leadership and you're not ready. And I think as that relates to hip-hop, I think some of them are given so much power and they're given that microphone, that freedom of speech that sometimes I believe is taken for granted. . . But then there's a whole lot of other emcee's, poets that you know, I just could really fall in love with the first time I hear them because they have so much to say that's of weight. And I'm the type of person that

I'm completely into lyrical content and I want to be taken on a journey or I want to be taught something or . . . you know . . . I just want to feel different after I hear the song and that doesn't mean I want to feel worse about my circumstance or even my brother or my sister's circumstance because they haven't met up to the expectations of who that person is rapping on the mic. "You don't have this. You don't have that. I got this. I own everything in the world." You know it becomes a little taxing so what I've done is made it a responsibility of my own . . . when I hear an emcee that's kicking something that's worth hearing. . . I make sure that whenever I have the light on me, no pun intended, that I say their name. That I share that Iman, out of Chicago, is like one of the best female emcees ever to hit the microphone and teaches at the same time. Slice and you know she's just so precise with it. So I like to give those acknowledgments.

**Dr. Chavis**: That's great. And you know I think one of the reasons why I'm optimistic despite all the stuff that's going on with the young men of our communities . . . some of it is kinda awful, but amidst the depth of the negativity, I think we can resurrect not only something that's positive, but I think people can be turned around. In other words, I believe in redemption. I don't think anyone is outside the pale of being redeemed. But you gotta… at some point, you gotta want to be redeemed and realize that if by God's grace you become redeemed, you just can't walk away from everybody else. The only thing I did not like about the movie Twelve Years A

Slave was how it ended. There's no way in the world if I was held illegally as a slave and got a chance to walk away that I would walk away and leave my other brothers and sisters in slavery. I'd get something up to have a stage or some kind of escape or in other words when you experience something you just can't walk away from it; and a lot of times stuff is going on in our communities where some of us are privileged to escape…

**Lyte**: And never come back.

**Dr. Chavis**: Our communities need us . . . we should lead not leave. We got people that are leaving the community rather than leading the community. And to me, if you, by God's grace, have an experience that can be shared . . . and I find the hunger and the thirst among the young lyricists . . . I think they really want to know. I think they do want to connect. But they do need nurturing. I think they need support. They need to be embraced. There are a lot of pointing fingers going on. There are a lot of player haters out here. Just player hate on the whole culture. But that does not mean we cannot be self-critical for the betterment. We should always try to improve whatever it is we do. No one is perfect. But we're striving toward that perfection. That's why I said to you the other day "I'm in the resurrection business."

**Lyte**: I love that. Resurrection business. Bring'em up! Bring'em up. . . 'cause that's really what it's about, taking them to a higher level of consciousness. You spoke of self-destruction and young people being in a state of needing more, but also missing out on that point where the consciousness sets in due to not enough exposure, someone not taking their hand and saying "Let me show you this. Let me show you that. Let me show you who Dr. Ben Chavis is and what he's done for the movement and continues to do." Within that missing link, we're seeing violence perpetuated across the nation, specifically in Chicago. What are your feelings about that?

**Dr. Chavis**: I believe the whole situation in Chicago can be turned around, but not from the outside putting a cop on every corner. It has to come from within. The problem comes from within; the solution has to come from within. I think that inside of every problem is its own solution. And I think that the solution to young brothers killing each other in Chicago will come from them. So what would bring that moment? What's the pivot that will cause that to happen? I think that if the young people in Chicago are constantly told that this is a downward spiral it will become a self-fulfilling prophecy where people become hopeless in themselves; Lifeless for themselves. And so I think that in the mix of that situation I guarantee you, and this is where I come to hip-hop. A lot of hip-hop heads are on those street corners vibing. I think that... look at all the talent that has come out of Chicago. A lot of times the talent has to leave 'cause if they stay they may not make it. I've talked to a lot of artists "Man I had to get out." And I understand that. But the truth of the matter is when we . . . you can't change the world Lyte; if I ain't changing the street I live on. I can't change somebody else's family, if I ain't changing my own family.

**Lyte**: Yeah that's the testament.

**Dr. Chavis**: I have to attend to my kid at the same time, attend to the community's kids. It's not either or. You have to do both and I think sometimes we'll select. I want to ask you a question Lyte, because to me, you just haven't survived, you have transcended a lot of the pitfalls that's happened to even a lot of the sisters in hip-hop. And again, that's why I support Hip-Hop sisters. But I just want to go over something with you, tell me what has contributed, not just to your survival, but what has contributed to, who you are today and the glow that you still have?

**Lyte**: The glow? Hmm. I would have to first say my mother for introducing me to God. You know, God. But when someone close to you can explain why it is that we're here and what we're here to do and that everyone has a purpose and a mission and just instilling that drive and belief in myself that I can accomplish anything . . . and I tend to believe that we're all born with positive charge and negative charge. Some people's negative is more than their positive. So no matter how much positivity you give to them, you're still on an uphill climb for them to see the good, for them to be optimistic to see the glass half full as opposed to half empty. And then you have people who thank God...the positivity that was instilled in me even when there's adversity, even when I see those pitfalls, and occasionally might fall in one. It doesn't take me long to get up out of it because I believe that God will get me out of it. So, I would have to say that she, my mother, has been the force that keeps me going even when everything else says that you should sit down. That it's time to just, you know, take on the weight of the world and I don't believe that that's the route that I have to go. So within that, there's a whole bunch of other factors, aligning yourself with the right people, keeping people around you that bring positive energy that can help you see things that you may not see.

**Dr. Chavis**: But, do you pass on the strength of your mother that you have just described, do you pass that on to other sisters?

**Lyte**: I believe I pass it on to the world. She was once a talented, and she's still talented, but I mean she wrote plays in school; she acted in theatre; she wrote poetry and so now she is my muse. I am from her seed and I am able to now go out into the world and do all of what she had intended to do prior to having me. So, I think with Hip Hop Sisters, the foundation, we're able to touch a lot of young girls in a positive way, an empowering way, to encourage them to be more and expect more.

**Dr. Chavis**: Yeah, I think that's so important. Most public schools today, Chicago, LA, New York, Atlanta, St. Louis, Detroit, Philly . . .they're taking music education . . . art education . . .out of public schools. One would have to ask, what is going on with that. In the hood, people play the dozens, people talk about everybody's mama, and I was so pleased just to let you run about the role that your mother played in your life, still plays in your life, and now the role that you play in other women's lives and men, just the whole of humanity. I, personally, feel that we need each other. I think sometimes we live in such a divisive society; where males are pitted off against females, females are pitted off against males, the whole racial divide, the sexual orientation divide. There's so many divides. I think when I was in prison for the Willimgton Ten, a white female, religion reporter, sent me a letter with some questions and one of the questions was, what have you learned? What was the most significant thing you've learned while you were incarcerated? I thought about it. I wrote her a 21-page letter to the Charlotte Observer, religious section, and my answer was, what I've learned while I was incarcerated was about the importance of the oneness of humanity. Now people say, "Ben, what's wrong with you, you're crazy, in prison, you're a victim of racism and you're talking about some oneness of humanity? Have you gone soft?" But, I had to be honest, that's how I felt and I still write about that occasionally and in other words it's not so much what makes us different. It is what unites us that is one of the most important aspects of life.

**Lyte**: What are the similarities.

**Dr. Chavis**: Right. What, when and how do I define you as my comrade in the struggle; that I would die for you and you would die for me. But more importantly, and this was my little debate . . . I don't believe in revolutionary suicide. I believe that the revolution is supposed to be about living life to its fullest manifestation.

**Lyte**: Right because you must want to do your work.

**Dr. Chavis**: That's right. So, when people say I'll die for you. No, don't die for me, LIVE for me, live for yourself. And so, I want to ask you, what do you live for today?

**Lyte**: I live to inspire by any means necessary. So if that's through books, through speaking, through music, which is still a love of mine. I work on songs and lyrics all the time. You know, people ask me, "when are you coming out with something new?" . . .I don't know . . .I don't really create it with the intention of a time or date for it to be released. I just do it because it's in my heart. And I want people to be where I am. It's funny when I hear people either . . .not hear, but see on twitter . . .going back and forth on who's the best female MC and you know, "MC Lyte is the greatest lyricist" and these are young people saying this, so I wonder what are they basing that on, in terms of the time frame of when they listened. It's so funny because to me, you know, Paper Thin and all of those earlier hits of mine in the early 80s, excuse me, late 80s, early 90s . . . I was just talking. And that's what I feel like we kinda need to get back to, making a stance, say something. I remember being in the studio in the late 90s working on a record and this producer said to me, "Don't make one line go into the next. Kinda make it abstract." And I think that's what we have today, a bunch of abstract rhymes, which is great . . .but then also I think to be able to tell a story and have people feel what you feel and inspire them to go out and be bigger and better than who they are and who they have yet to become. I take a lot of pride and responsibility in being able to expose an MC or a writer or a poet or just a person who doesn't aspire to be any of those . . . but I like the idea of being able to give them thought and ideas that they can then take and make them their own.

**Dr. Chavis**: You know what I would love to do? I want to… We should write something together.

**Lyte**: We should do that.

**Dr. Chavis**: We should say something to the world.

**Lyte**: That would be awesome. That would be awesome. You know what I love, when I hear you speak . . . whether it's doing a speech or just speaking amongst friends . . .it's just the care. I love the amount of care and patience that you put into conveying a message. You don't haphazardly use words and you're very purposeful with the message that you're getting across and in the words that you choose. . . I really love that about you.

**Dr. Chavis**: Well thank you, thank you. Well, I get inspired by you.

**Lyte**: Ha!

**Dr. Chavis**: James ***Bowen*** was a close friend of mine. He used to tell me, he was a great writer, he said, "Ben, the pen is mightier than the sword." So I always like to take care of what I write, of what I say. I don't like to be misunderstood. But now, I've always been this way. I've been in situations where I've had to suppress how I feel.

**Lyte**: I wanted to ask you . . .because you are a father of 6?

**Dr. Chavis**: 8.

**Lyte**: 8.

**Dr. Chavis**: 4 boys, 4 girls.

**Lyte**: 4 boys, 4 girls. What is the importance, or should I say, what has been the most life-altering aspect of having children?

**Dr. Chavis**: What I think, when you are responsible, in part, because you know, you don't bring a person into this world by yourself; it takes a strong woman to bring a baby into this world. Even with the best of prenatal care and all the stuff that goes on, it takes a lot of strength to do that. But to answer your question, I think parental responsibility.... A lot of parents say, "Well, I don't want my child to go through what I had to go through." But in truth, I want my children to be conscious and I have found out that if I just put them on automatic pilot, they won't get it. So, part of the answer to the question you've raised is that I have to at least take time with my own kids to make sure they know a little something about the movement. Now, they may not choose to be a minister, they may not choose to be a businessperson or whatever. But they would never say, "Well, my father died without at least taking time to tell me about the struggle." So, they get a fair amount of dosage from me about the movement. Now, I don't twist on their arms. I don't **require** them to . . .So, I know that's over a period of time. Now a couple of my sons, sometimes my daughter would say, *"Hey Dad, can I go with you"* . . .or *"what's that about; I saw this tweet"* or *"I saw this on Facebook"* or *"I saw this picture on Instagram,"* . . . *"What are you doing?"* You know, I like that kind of inquisition and interest because it shows me that they're thinking. I think that . . . I'm gonna go back to this oneness and humanity thing . . .I don't want my children to feel that they are better than other children. I want my children to have a sense of responsibility for their friends and their colleagues. But look at the world. I have a problem right now, knowing that there are a lot of children on the

border of the United States and Mexico, being stacked up like they're cattle. It makes me uncomfortable.

**Lyte**: Yeah, yeah, it does. I know exactly what you mean.

**Dr. Chavis**: You know, it makes me uncomfortable and sometimes I think, we as Black Americans, it's not that we become insensitive because we've been through a lot. But, this whole question of solidarity. You know, who are we in solidarity with, and what is the purpose? When we tried to dismantle apartheid in South Africa it was very clear, oh man we all going to tear down the apartheid. And I sometimes think we know what we are against but we aren't quite clear on what we are for.

**MC Lyte**: And how do we get clear?

**Dr. Chavis**: Through struggle... through self-expression. I'm a much better writer . . . the more I write the better I become. The more I speak, the better I become. If you would've met me

30 years ago, I mean I was just running it. I was a rhetorician.

**MC Lyte**: Rhetorician. You know, right…

**Dr. Chavis**: But, now I have had time and I take care because I, not, only want to make sure I am being accurate when I say…I want people again not to just hear what I'm saying . . . but I want you to feel what I'm saying.

**Lyte**: Exactly.

**Dr. Chavis**: And then a lot of times there are brothers and sisters out there who are born and they get no attention. So whenever I get that mic, I want to make sure that I say something with that mic. The mic is powerful.

**Lyte**: Oh, absolutely. You want to say something that is going to touch someone in a special kind of way, so that they're never the same. Something has got to change

**Dr. Chavis**: Let me tell you a true story. I know the time is short and we got to get this done, but, the movie Belly, that last scene. You know for Hype Williams, that was his only full-length movie. He shot it like a two-hour video. DMX is there, holding a gun on me, and my job in the movie, as the preacher, is to talk him out of shooting me. No matter what hood I go into . . . not only in the United States . . . in Brazil or in the Caribbean . . .young people say: that's the dude from Belly. And they would memorize those lines. I know you were coming . . .you represent the fire. A generation that wants more, but sometimes we engage in things that are not good. And then it's this line: the most precious thing is a black woman. That's in that line.

**Lyte**: Who wrote that script?

**Dr. Chavis**: Hype Williams.

**Lyte**: Hype Williams wrote the script as well?

**Dr. Chavis**: Yeah, yeah.

**Lyte**: He's a very poignant brother in our generation and he is still doing videos. So he has kind of transcended what he's known for into a whole new spectrum. There are so many of our young brothers who are incarcerated today and with you having been detained . . .how long were you imprisoned?

**Dr. Chavis**: I actually served four and one-half years straight in prison.

**Lyte**: So with that in mind, with what it is these guys are facing . . .what our young men are facing today, with being jailed for crimes that at some point may have been committed, but so many more are being detained for nothing less than j walking for that matter. How does that make you feel?

**Dr. Chavis**: Well, I think the whole mass incarceration ...disproportionate incarceration of black males . . .in 1972 there was a serious dysfunctionality of our system. I think our criminal justice system is appropriately named. The system itself is criminal. But, I say that since I went to prison, and I'm going to say this to young brothers. Don't seek to go to prison to gain something. It's very difficult . . .it's not impossible . . . but you can gain more by not going to jail…by not going to prison. I'm saying that because there's a little myth out there that you get a rep and come out stronger, if you went to the joint. No. Most people come out weaker. Unless, see before I went, I made a decision. I was never going to serve time. I was going to make time serve the cause of our people. So I woke up with that, I went to sleep, said my prayers constantly. The human being adjusts to an environment. So whenever you are incarcerated they give you all kinds of tests.

**Lyte**: Written tests?

**Dr. Chavis**: Written tests, psychological analysis tests. So I had been in the prison about eight months and they called me to the office in central prison and said that I needed to have a psychological test. I said okay since this is what y'all require. So this psychiatrist says Reverend Chavis we have a few questions we want to ask you. And the first question was: What did you dream about last night? And I said escaping.

**Lyte**: No you didn't.

**Dr. Chavis**: Yes I did. He says I'm going to ask you this again. What did you dream about last night? Escaping. I said you a psychiatrist right? If I would've told you I had a good dream, while locked up in this prison. . . one . . . *you* need to be on the couch. That's unhealthy. I dream about escaping, I think about escaping. And the first opportunity I get I am going to escape.

**Lyte**: Is that what you said?

**Dr. Chavis**: That's exactly what I said.

**Lyte**: Did they give you more time?

**Dr. Chavis**: No, they didn't give me more time, but they said, "don't let this Negro get in a situation." Naaah . . .they didn't want me to influence other inmates, so I stayed in a lot of isolation cells.

**Lyte**: Is that right?

**Dr. Chavis**: Yeah.

**Lyte**: What is that experience like?

**Dr. Chavis**: Well isolation . . . well again, I knew I was in prison . . . but I never accepted it. See a lot of times we accept a situation and then we start adapting to our acceptance. I never accepted, so I never adapted. Whether I was in a prison cell with twenty guys or in a cell by myself. I never adapted. Because, I had made up my mind that I'm not going to let this be my permanent reality. I had a thirty-four year prison sentence as a member of the Wilmington, North Carolina Ten.

**Lyte**: That's what I was going to ask you, of the 34 years; you were released four and one half years later?

**Dr. Chavis**: Well, it took ten years of litigation to overturn the conviction, and then took another thirty years for the state of North Carolina to issue a pardon of innocence. So it was a forty-year struggle to clear our names totally. We finally got it done thanks to the National Newspaper Publishers Association, thanks to the United Church of Christ, thanks to the NAACP, thanks to the National

Wilmington Defense Committee. Thanks to the National *Alliance Against* Racist and Political *Repression (NAARPR)*. Angela Davis worked very hard, you know, struggle hard. So the Wilmington Ten case is symptomatic. I don't want people to see the Wilmington Ten case as an exceptional case. It was symptomatic of the racism in the criminal justice system, discrimination, and also they want to give you the opportunity to conform. And then they got you. That's why the recidivism rate is so high.

**Lyte**: Right, because they want to go back.

**Dr. Chavis**: Some brothers want to go back. They can't deal with being free; they got to go back. The idea in some cases is, somebody going to feed me, somebody tell me when to go to sleep, somebody tell me when to wake up, somebody to tell me when to raise up, somebody to tell me when to go take a shower. And if you get institutionalized…

**Lyte**: Then it's over.

**Dr. Chavis**: Then they got you.

**Lyte**: Before you were incarcerated, what exactly happened?

**Dr. Chavis**: There was a racial riot in Wilmington, North Carolina in February of 1971 because of the desegregation of schools. One year later, in March of 1972, Wilmington, North Carolina and the county where we were located indicted sixteen people. First, it was the Wilmington 16 and of the original sixteen, fourteen were teenagers, high school students;

16, 17, 18 years old, one white woman, and myself.

**Lyte**: And what exactly did you do? You rioted?

**Dr. Chavis**: No, we didn't riot. I was a student organizer. I was the civil rights movement builder in Wilmington. And we were organizing in a local black church. The Klu Klux Klan and a pile of military white supremacists groups called the Rights of White People attacked us in the church. Keep in mind this is in 1971, Richard Nixon is the president, "law and order."

So we called down to the local police department and said we would like some law and order, some police protection in our own community, our own church. We are trying to mobilize a peaceful protest to get the schools situation straight where black kids can get a good education. The Chief of Police. . . his name was *Williamson* . . . says "you're an outside agitator. Close up that church stop having these meetings and the Klan won't have nothing to shoot at." We said "no, we're not closing up the church. I'm not leaving. I'm not an outside agitator and

Wilmington is already agitated." The racism in the schools is what agitated the people. I was the organizer of the movement. So of the sixteen people that were originally indicted, ten were actually brought to trial on two charges; Allegedly burning down a white grocery store called Mike's Grocery Store, and when the store caught on fire, allegedly police and firemen were shot at. So we were unjustly charged with the arson of the store and falsely accused of shooting at policemen and firemen. On those two charges, collectively the ten of us were sentenced to 282 years in prison. I had the longest of the ten. I had a thirty-four year sentence. The others had twenty, twenty-two, twenty-six years.

**Lyte**: And that was because you were an organizer?

**Dr. Chavis**: It was because I was the leader of the Wilmington 10. I don't deny that I was a leader. That's why I sat there.

**Lyte**: You know when I see and hear of leadership of something so righteous for the people, for the community . . . there's such a lack of it now. Like really . . . if we were to line up all of the soldiers who were ready to lead, it would be your generation. I can't really think of anyone from my generation who is willing to take a stand in that capacity.

**Dr. Chavis**: Well I think that your generation certainly has the capacity.

**Lyte**: Absolutely.

**Dr. Chavis**: To rise to the occasion . . .but they have to be summoned. Keep in mind my generation was summoned. Dr. King's generation opened the doors. My generation went through the doors and we . . .there's no way in the world that someone died to get the right to vote and we not going to vote. There's no way in the world somebody died to get the schools desegregated and we going to allow these people to mistreat us. Naah. So quite frankly, I was asked recently on BBC to self describe. I am a seasoned militant in my sixties. I'm seasoned, I'm not wild, I'm not crazy. I have grown very disciplined over a period of time. Because to me you struggle to win, you just don't struggle to struggle. We have to win victories.

**Lyte**: There has to be an upside. You know who I do think of? I think of Tupac.

**Dr. Chavis**: Tupac. I knew Tupac. That was my man. And I knew his mother Afeni too. A strong woman. Afeni Shakur.

**Lyte**: I wonder at this point and time if he'd still been alive what would be his mission?

**Dr. Chavis**: I think if Tupac Shakur was alive today, he'd probably be in the congress.

Representing something urban, He'd be spitting truth in the halls of congress.

**Lyte**: He…when you talked about writing and speaking and you learn more about yourself, I think, as a writer . . . I don't know if a lot of musicians or especially, in hip-hop even know this . . . but he shared that his works came out of writing. It wasn't out of listening to music. It was purely him and that pen and later he put it to music. This was so the music wouldn't influence which direction he was going.

**Dr. Chavis**: And Tupac was a dramatic artist. Tupac knew the culture of arts. He wasn't one-dimensional. And that's why by the time he put that pen and that lyric together it had a certain cadence. And people try to copy Tupac. I tell artists all the time . . .be yourself. Be your God given self.

**Lyte**: Because no one else can do it.

**Dr. Chavis**: That's right.

**Lyte**: This is great. This is just part one. We need to do part two.

**Dr. Chavis**: We're going to do many parts.

**Lyte**: Thank you so, so much.

**Dr. Chavis**: And Lyte I need to say something about your name. You are the Lyte of the world.

**Lyte**: Thank you so much. It's because of you that I can see.

**Dr. Chavis**: It's because of you that I can celebrate the illumination you have brought to the world and continue to bring to the world. That's what's so good about it. We ain't finished yet.

**Lyte**: Thank you. Keep leading us.

## Join the Movement:
### www.hiphopsistersnetwork.org

**About Hip-Hop Sisters Network**
Founded by MC Lyte, the legendary lyricist and iconic hip-hop pioneer, Hip Hop Sisters Network is a non-profit organization that promotes positive images of women of ethnic diversity, bringing leaders from the world of Hip Hop, the entertainment industry, and the corporate world.

Celebrity advisory board members include Faith Evans, Ledisi, Jada Pinkett Smith, Chilli, Russell Simmons, Cheryl "Salt" James,

Malinda Williams, Kelly Price, Malcolm Jamal Warner, and Dr. Benjamin Chavis.

# #EDUCATEOURMEN

**#EducateOURMen** is the signature education initiative of the Hip Hop Sisters Foundation that aims to support and develop African-American males by: providing need-based scholarships to obtain undergraduate degrees primarily from HBCUs; providing access to career and personal mentoring; and increasing cultural education and social responsibility.

Each year since it's inception, Hip Hop Sisters Foundation has presented youth with full college scholarships during the Soul Train Music Awards.

## About Dr. Benjamin F. Chavis, Jr.

Civil Rights Activist, Educator, Author, and Philanthropist Dr. Chavis serves as the President and CEO of the National Newspaper Publishers Association and President and CEO of the Hip-Hop Summit Action Network (HSAN). His fight for civil rights and justice began at twelve-year-old when young Chavis effectively desegregated his hometown's whites-only public library. Chavis went on to lead, organized and enforce change nationally. Chavis served under Rev. Dr. Martin Luther King Jr. as youth coordinator of the SCLC. He was appointed Field Officer in the United Church of Christ Commission for Racial Justice. In 1968 he was appointed Southern Regional Program Director of the 1.7

million member United Church of Christ Commission for Racial Justice (UCC-CRJ). In 1985, he was named the Executive Director and CEO of the UCC-CRJ. In 1988, Dr. Chavis was elected Vice President of the National Council of Churches.

In 1993, Dr. Chavis became the youngest Executive Director and CEO of the National Association for the Advancement of Colored People (NAACP). In 1995, Chavis with other civil rights leaders founded the National African American Leadership Summit (NAALS) and served as Executive Director and CEO of NAALS from 1995 to 1997. In 1995, NAALS appointed Dr. Chavis to serve as the National Director of the Million Man March. In 2001, Dr. Chavis and Russell Simmons Co-founded the Hip-Hop Summit Action

Network. In 2013, Chavis launched his national lecture series, traveling to towns, Universities, and public forums uplifting and encouraging unity.

Dr. Chavis has authored books and other publications including: An American Political Prisoner Appeals for Human Rights, Psalms from Prison, Toxic Waste and Race in the United States of America: A National Report on the Racial and Socioeconomic Characteristics of Communities with Hazardous Waste Sites, Pastoral Letter on Contemporary Racism and the Role of the Church, and The National Agenda: Public Policy Issues, Analyses, And Programmatic Plans of Action (2000-2008).

## About MC Lyte

First African American female President of the Los Angeles Chapter of the Recording Academy (Grammy Organization) is the first of many firsts. Lyricist, pioneer, icon, inspirational speaker, veteran, philanthropist, and entrepreneur describe one of the most prolific and well-respected female Hip Hop artists of our time: **Lana "MC Lyte" Moorer**. A pioneer in the industry, she opened the door for future female Hip Hop artists by daring to do what had never been done while doing something she loved. A role model to women and respected by men everywhere, Lyte never compromises who she is and consistently displays that a woman can turn heads fully clothed! Whenever possible, **Lyte,** as she is affectionately known by her inner circle, enjoys traveling across the nation to use her expertise and story of success to motivate others to take ownership of the world around them while striving to be the best they can possibly be.

Author of "**Unstoppable: Igniting the Power Within to Achieve Your Greatest Potential**," and "**Living in the Lyte: Lessons in Life, Love, and Living**," **MC Lyte** is the Founder/Chairman of Hip Hop Sisters Foundation, Inc. the President/CEO of Sunni Gyrl, Inc., a global entertainment firm, the immediate past President of the Los Angeles Chapter of the Recording Academy (Grammy Organization) and she is also a proud honorary member of Sigma Gamma Rho Sorority, Inc.